Gifts from a Jar

Muffins, Breads & Scones

Gift Giving Made Easy 2

White Chocolate Chunk Muffins 3

Cranberry Pecan Muffins 5

Date Nut Bread 7

Cranberry Corn Bread 9

Fruity Gingerbread Muffins 11

Lemon Raisin Quick Bread 13

English-Style Scones 15

Applesauce-Spice Bread 33

Chocolate Macadamia Nut Muffins 35

Currant Scones 37

Strawberry Muffins 39

Apple Raisin Muffins 41

Apricot-Cranberry Bread 43

Pumpkin Chocolate Chip Muffins 45

Peanut Butter Chocolate Chip Loaves 47

Gift Giving Made Easy

Show your friends and family just how much you care by giving them a beautiful homemade gift jar filled with the ingredients to bake delicious muffins, breads and scones.

Keep the following tips in mind when preparing your gift jars:

- Always use a food-safe jar or container with an airtight lid. Make sure the jar or container is completely dry before filling it with ingredients.
- Use the jar size called for in the recipe.
- Measure all the ingredients accurately.
- For ease in filling, use a wide mouth jar if possible. Layer the ingredients into the jar using a ¼-cup dry measuring cup or the largest spoon that fits through the mouth of the jar.
- For more attractive jars, divide ingredients with large amounts (1 cup or more) into 2 layers.
- Fine ingredients such as flour and granulated sugar are best layered on the bottom of the jar, or on top of more compact ingredients, such as oats and brown sugar. When placed on top of loosely layered ingredients, such as chocolate chips or nuts, flour and granulated sugar tend to cover up those loosely layered ingredients.
- After the jar is filled, make sure to replace the lid securely. Then, tear out the corresponding gift tag from this book. Cover the top of the jar with a 9- or 10-inch circle of fabric. Tie the fabric and the gift tag onto the jar with raffia, ribbon, satin cord, string, yarn or lace.

White Chocolate Chunk Muffin Mix

- 2½ cups all-purpose flour
- 1½ cups chopped white chocolate chunks or chips
- 1 cup packed brown sugar
- ⅓ cup unsweetened cocoa powder
- 2 teaspoons baking soda
- ½ teaspoon salt

1. Layer ingredients attractively in any order in 1-quart food storage jar with tight-fitting lid. Pack ingredients down slightly before adding another layer.

2. Cover top of jar with fabric; attach gift tag with raffia or ribbon.

Makes one (1-quart) jar

White Chocolate Chunk Muffins

1 jar White Chocolate Chunk Muffin Mix
1⅓ cups buttermilk
6 tablespoons butter, melted
2 eggs, beaten
1½ teaspoons vanilla

1. Preheat oven to 400°F. Grease or paper-line 18 regular-size (2½-inch) muffin cups.

2. Pour contents of jar into large bowl. Combine buttermilk, butter, eggs and vanilla in small bowl until blended; stir into jar mixture just until moistened. Spoon evenly into prepared muffin cups, filling about ⅔ full.

3. Bake 16 to 18 minutes or until toothpick inserted in centers comes out clean. Cool in pans on wire racks 5 minutes; remove from pans and cool 10 minutes on wire racks. *Makes 18 muffins*

Cranberry Pecan Muffin Mix

1¾ cups all-purpose flour
1 cup dried cranberries
¾ cup chopped pecans
½ cup packed light brown sugar
2½ teaspoons baking powder
½ teaspoon salt

1. Layer ingredients attractively in any order in 1-quart food storage jar with tight-fitting lid. Pack ingredients down slightly before adding another layer.

2. Cover top of jar with fabric; attach gift tag with raffia or ribbon.

Makes one (1-quart) jar

Cranberry Pecan Muffins

1 jar Cranberry Pecan Muffin Mix
¾ cup milk
¼ cup (½ stick) butter, melted
1 egg, beaten

1. Preheat oven to 400°F. Grease or paper-line 12 regular-size (2½-inch) muffin cups.

2. Pour contents of jar into large bowl. Combine milk, butter and egg in small bowl until blended; stir into jar mixture just until moistened. Spoon evenly into prepared muffin cups.

3. Bake 16 to 18 minutes or until toothpick inserted into centers comes out clean. Cool in pan on wire rack 5 minutes; remove from pan and cool completely on wire rack. *Makes 12 muffins*

Date Nut Bread Mix

2 cups all-purpose flour
1 cup chopped dates
1 cup toasted chopped walnuts
½ cup packed light brown sugar
1 tablespoon baking powder
½ teaspoon salt
½ teaspoon ground cinnamon

1. Layer ingredients attractively in any order in 1-quart food storage jar with tight-fitting lid. Pack ingredients down slightly before adding another layer.

2. Cover top of jar with fabric; attach gift tag with raffia or ribbon.

Makes one (1-quart) jar

Date Nut Bread

1 jar Date Nut Bread Mix
¼ cup (½ stick) butter
1¼ cups milk
1 egg

1. Preheat oven to 375°F. Spray 9×5-inch loaf pan with nonstick cooking spray.

2. Pour contents of jar into large bowl. Cut in butter with pastry blender or two knives until mixture resembles fine crumbs. Beat milk and egg in small bowl until well blended. Add to jar mixture; stir just until moistened. Pour into prepared pan.

3. Bake 45 to 50 minutes or until toothpick inserted into center comes out clean. Cool in pan on wire rack 10 minutes; remove from pan and cool completely on wire rack. *Makes 1 loaf*

Cranberry Corn Bread Mix

1½ cups all-purpose flour
1 cup yellow cornmeal
1 cup dried cranberries
½ cup sugar
2 teaspoons baking powder
½ teaspoon baking soda
½ teaspoon salt

1. Layer ingredients attractively in any order in 1-quart food storage jar with tight-fitting lid. Pack ingredients down slightly before adding another layer.

2. Cover top of jar with fabric; attach gift tag with raffia or ribbon.

Makes one (1-quart) jar

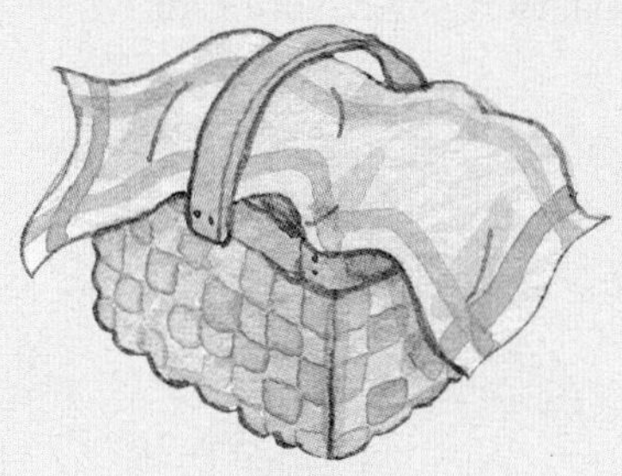

Cranberry Corn Bread

- 1 jar Cranberry Corn Bread Mix
- ½ cup shortening
- 1⅓ cups buttermilk
- 2 eggs

1. Preheat oven to 350°F. Spray 8½×4½-inch loaf pan with nonstick cooking spray.

2. Pour contents of jar into large bowl. Cut in shortening with pastry blender or two knives until mixture resembles coarse crumbs. Beat buttermilk and eggs in small bowl until blended. Add to shortening mixture; stir until mixture forms stiff batter. (Batter will be lumpy.) Pour into prepared pan, spreading evenly and removing any air bubbles.

3. Bake 45 to 50 minutes or until toothpick inserted into center comes out clean. Cool in pan on wire rack 10 minutes; remove from pan and cool 10 minutes longer. Serve warm. *Makes 1 loaf*

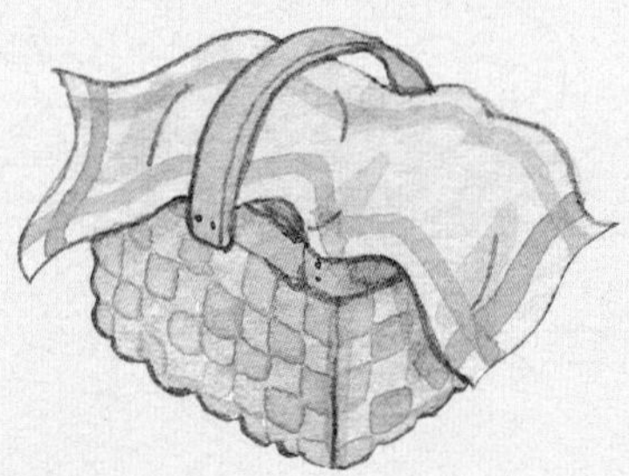

Fruity Gingerbread Muffin Mix

- 1¾ cups all-purpose flour
- 1 cup chopped dried mixed fruit bits
- 1 cup chopped nuts
- ⅓ cup sugar
- 2 teaspoons baking powder
- ¾ teaspoon ground ginger
- ¼ teaspoon salt
- ¼ teaspoon baking soda
- ¼ teaspoon ground cinnamon

1. Layer ingredients attractively in any order in 1-quart food storage jar with tight-fitting lid. Pack ingredients down slightly before adding another layer.

2. Cover top of jar with fabric; attach gift tag with raffia or ribbon.

Makes one (1-quart) jar

Fruity Gingerbread Muffins

- 1 jar Fruity Gingerbread Muffin Mix
- ½ cup milk
- ⅓ cup vegetable oil
- ¼ cup light molasses
- 1 egg

1. Preheat oven to 375°F. Grease or paper-line 12 regular-size (2½-inch) muffin cups.

2. Pour contents of jar into large bowl. Combine milk, oil, molasses and egg in medium bowl. Stir milk mixture into flour mixture just until moistened. Spoon evenly into prepared muffin cups, filling ⅔ full.

3. Bake 15 to 18 minutes or until toothpick inserted into centers comes out clean. Remove from pan; cool on wire rack 10 minutes. Serve warm or cold. *Makes 12 muffins*

Lemon Raisin Quick Bread Mix

- 2 cups all-purpose flour
- 1 cup raisins
- ¾ cup chopped walnuts
- ⅓ cup packed brown sugar
- 2 teaspoons baking powder
- ½ teaspoon baking soda
- ¼ teaspoon salt

1. Layer ingredients attractively in any order in 1-quart food storage jar with tight-fitting lid. Pack ingredients down slightly before adding another layer.

2. Cover top of jar with fabric; attach gift tag with raffia or ribbon.

Makes one (1-quart) jar

Lemon Raisin Quick Bread

- 1 jar Lemon Raisin Quick Bread Mix
- 1½ cups lemon-flavored yogurt (not artificially sweetened)
- ¼ cup butter, melted and slightly cooled
- 1 egg

1. Preheat oven to 350°F. Spray 8½×4½-inch loaf pan with nonstick cooking spray.

2. Pour contents of jar into large bowl. Combine yogurt, butter and egg in small bowl until blended; stir into jar mixture just until moistened. Pour evenly into prepared pan and smooth top.

3. Bake 45 to 50 minutes or until toothpick inserted into center comes out clean. Cool in pan on wire rack 30 minutes; remove from pan and cool completely on wire rack. *Makes 1 loaf*

English-Style Scone Mix

- 3 cups all-purpose flour
- ¾ cup golden raisins
- ¾ cup finely chopped pitted dates
- 1 tablespoon baking powder
- ¼ teaspoon salt

1. Layer ingredients attractively in any order in 1-quart food storage jar with tight-fitting lid.

2. Cover top of jar with fabric; attach gift tag with raffia or ribbon.

Makes one (1-quart) jar

English-Style Scones

1 jar English-Style Scone Mix
6 tablespoons cold butter
4 eggs, divided
¾ cup heavy cream
2 teaspoons vanilla
1 teaspoon water

1. Preheat oven to 375°F. Grease two cookie sheets.

2. Pour contents of jar into large bowl. Add butter; blend with pastry blender or two knives until mixture resembles coarse crumbs. Beat 3 eggs, cream and vanilla in small bowl. Add to flour mixture; mix just until ingredients are moistened. Knead dough several times on lightly floured surface. Divide dough in half; place each half on prepared cookie sheet and pat into 6-inch circle (about 1 inch thick).

3. With sharp, wet knife, gently score each circle of dough into six wedges, cutting ¾ of the way into dough. Beat remaining egg with water; brush lightly over dough. Bake 18 to 20 minutes or until golden brown. Cool 5 minutes on wire rack. Cut into wedges. Serve warm with marmalade and whipped cream.

Makes 12 scones

Cranberry Pecan Muffins

1 jar Cranberry Pecan Muffin Mix
¾ cup milk
¼ cup (½ stick) butter, melted
1 egg, beaten

1. Preheat oven to 400°F. Grease or paper-line 12 regular-size (2½-inch) muffin cups.

2. Pour contents of jar into large bowl. Combine milk, butter and egg in small bowl until blended; stir into jar mixture just until moistened. Spoon evenly into prepared muffin cups.

3. Bake 14 to 16 minutes or until toothpick inserted into centers comes out clean. Cool in pan on wire rack 5 minutes; remove from pan and cool completely on wire rack.

Makes 12 muffins

White Chocolate Chunk Muffins

1 jar White Chocolate Chunk Muffin Mix
1⅓ cups buttermilk
6 tablespoons butter, melted
2 eggs, beaten
1½ teaspoons vanilla

1. Preheat oven to 400°F. Grease or paper-line 18 regular-size (2½-inch) muffin cups.

2. Pour contents of jar into large bowl. Combine buttermilk, butter, eggs and vanilla in small bowl until blended; stir into jar mixture just until moistened. Spoon evenly into prepared muffin cups, filling about ⅔ full.

3. Bake 16 to 18 minutes or until toothpick inserted into centers comes out clean. Cool in pans on wire racks 5 minutes; remove from pans and cool 10 minutes on wire racks.

Makes 18 muffins

Cranberry Pecan Muffins

1 jar Cranberry Pecan Muffin Mix
¾ cup milk
¼ cup (½ stick) butter, melted
1 egg, beaten

1. Preheat oven to 400°F. Grease or paper-line 12 regular-size (2½-inch) muffin cups.

2. Pour contents of jar into large bowl. Combine milk, butter and egg in small bowl until blended; stir into jar mixture just until moistened. Spoon evenly into prepared muffin cups.

3. Bake 14 to 16 minutes or until toothpick inserted into centers comes out clean. Cool in pan on wire rack 5 minutes; remove from pan and cool completely on wire rack.

Makes 12 muffins

White Chocolate Chunk Muffins

1 jar White Chocolate Chunk Muffin Mix
1⅓ cups buttermilk
6 tablespoons butter, melted
2 eggs, beaten
1½ teaspoons vanilla

1. Preheat oven to 400°F. Grease or paper-line 18 regular-size (2½-inch) muffin cups.

2. Pour contents of jar into large bowl. Combine buttermilk, butter, eggs and vanilla in small bowl until blended; stir into jar mixture just until moistened. Spoon evenly into prepared muffin cups, filling about ⅔ full.

3. Bake 16 to 18 minutes or until toothpick inserted into centers comes out clean. Cool in pans on wire racks 5 minutes; remove from pans and cool 10 minutes on wire racks.

Makes 18 muffins

Cranberry Corn Bread

1 jar Cranberry Corn Bread Mix
½ cup shortening
1⅓ cups buttermilk
2 eggs

1. Preheat oven to 350°F. Spray 8½×4½-inch loaf pan with nonstick cooking spray.

2. Pour contents of jar into large bowl. Cut in shortening with pastry blender or two knives until mixture resembles coarse crumbs. Beat buttermilk and eggs in small bowl until blended. Add to shortening mixture; stir until mixture forms stiff batter. (Batter will be lumpy.) Pour into prepared pan, spreading evenly and removing any air bubbles.

3. Bake 45 to 50 minutes or until toothpick inserted into center comes out clean. Cool in pan on wire rack 10 minutes; remove from pan and cool 10 minutes longer. Serve warm.

Makes 1 loaf

Date Nut Bread

1 jar Date Nut Bread Mix
¼ cup (½ stick) butter
1¼ cups milk
1 egg

1. Preheat oven to 375°F. Spray 9×5-inch loaf pan with nonstick cooking spray.

2. Pour contents of jar into large bowl. Cut in butter with pastry blender or two knives until mixture resembles fine crumbs. Beat milk and egg in small bowl until well blended. Add to jar mixture; stir just until moistened. Pour into prepared pan.

3. Bake 45 to 50 minutes or until toothpick inserted into center comes out clean. Cool in pan on wire rack 10 minutes; remove from pan and cool completely on wire rack.

Makes 1 loaf

Cranberry Corn Bread

1 jar Cranberry Corn Bread Mix
½ cup shortening
1⅓ cups buttermilk
2 eggs

1. Preheat oven to 350°F. Spray 8½×4½-inch loaf pan with nonstick cooking spray.

2. Pour contents of jar into large bowl. Cut in shortening with pastry blender or two knives until mixture resembles coarse crumbs. Beat buttermilk and eggs in small bowl until blended. Add to shortening mixture; stir until mixture forms stiff batter. (Batter will be lumpy.) Pour into prepared pan, spreading evenly and removing any air bubbles.

3. Bake 45 to 50 minutes or until toothpick inserted into center comes out clean. Cool in pan on wire rack 10 minutes; remove from pan and cool 10 minutes longer. Serve warm.

Makes 1 loaf

Date Nut Bread

1 jar Date Nut Bread Mix
¼ cup (½ stick) butter
1¼ cups milk
1 egg

1. Preheat oven to 375°F. Spray 9×5-inch loaf pan with nonstick cooking spray.

2. Pour contents of jar into large bowl. Cut in butter with pastry blender or two knives until mixture resembles fine crumbs. Beat milk and egg in small bowl until well blended. Add to jar mixture; stir just until moistened. Pour into prepared pan.

3. Bake 45 to 50 minutes or until toothpick inserted into center comes out clean. Cool in pan on wire rack 10 minutes; remove from pan and cool completely on wire rack.

Makes 1 loaf

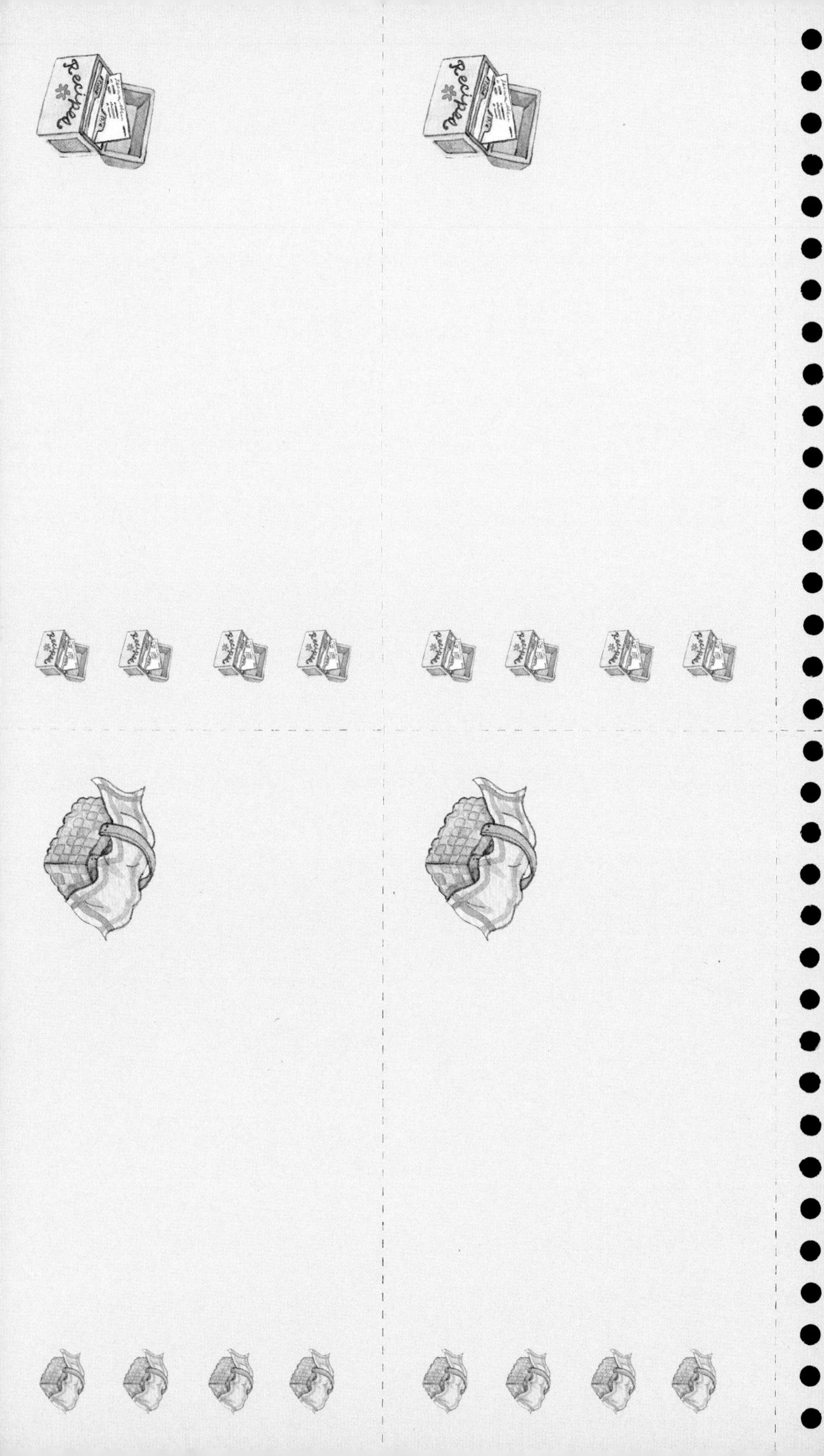

Lemon Raisin Quick Bread

- **1 jar Lemon Raisin Quick Bread Mix**
- **1½ cups lemon-flavored yogurt (not artificially sweetened)**
- **¼ cup butter, melted and slightly cooled**
- **1 egg**

1. Preheat oven to 350°F. Spray 8½×4½-inch loaf pan with nonstick cooking spray.

2. Pour contents of jar into large bowl. Combine yogurt, butter and egg in small bowl until blended; stir into jar mixture just until moistened. Pour evenly into prepared pan and smooth top.

3. Bake 45 to 50 minutes or until toothpick inserted into center comes out clean. Cool in pan on wire rack 30 minutes; remove from pan and cool completely on wire rack.

Makes 1 loaf

Fruity Gingerbread Muffins

- **1 jar Fruity Gingerbread Muffin Mix**
- **½ cup milk**
- **⅓ cup vegetable oil**
- **¼ cup light molasses**
- **1 egg**

1. Preheat oven to 375°F. Grease or paper-line 12 regular-size (2½-inch) muffin cups.

2. Pour contents of jar into large bowl. Combine milk, oil, molasses and egg in medium bowl. Stir milk mixture into flour mixture just until moistened. Spoon evenly into prepared muffin cups, filling ⅔ full.

3. Bake 15 to 18 minutes or until toothpick inserted into centers comes out clean. Remove from pan; cool on wire rack 10 minutes. Serve warm or cold. *Makes 12 muffins*

Lemon Raisin Quick Bread

- **1 jar Lemon Raisin Quick Bread Mix**
- **1½ cups lemon-flavored yogurt (not artificially sweetened)**
- **¼ cup butter, melted and slightly cooled**
- **1 egg**

1. Preheat oven to 350°F. Spray 8½×4½-inch loaf pan with nonstick cooking spray.

2. Pour contents of jar into large bowl. Combine yogurt, butter and egg in small bowl until blended; stir into jar mixture just until moistened. Pour evenly into prepared pan and smooth top.

3. Bake 45 to 50 minutes or until toothpick inserted into center comes out clean. Cool in pan on wire rack 30 minutes; remove from pan and cool completely on wire rack.

Makes 1 loaf

Fruity Gingerbread Muffins

- **1 jar Fruity Gingerbread Muffin Mix**
- **½ cup milk**
- **⅓ cup vegetable oil**
- **¼ cup light molasses**
- **1 egg**

1. Preheat oven to 375°F. Grease or paper-line 12 regular-size (2½-inch) muffin cups.

2. Pour contents of jar into large bowl. Combine milk, oil, molasses and egg in medium bowl. Stir milk mixture into flour mixture just until moistened. Spoon evenly into prepared muffin cups, filling ⅔ full.

3. Bake 15 to 18 minutes or until toothpick inserted into centers comes out clean. Remove from pan; cool on wire rack 10 minutes. Serve warm or cold. *Makes 12 muffins*

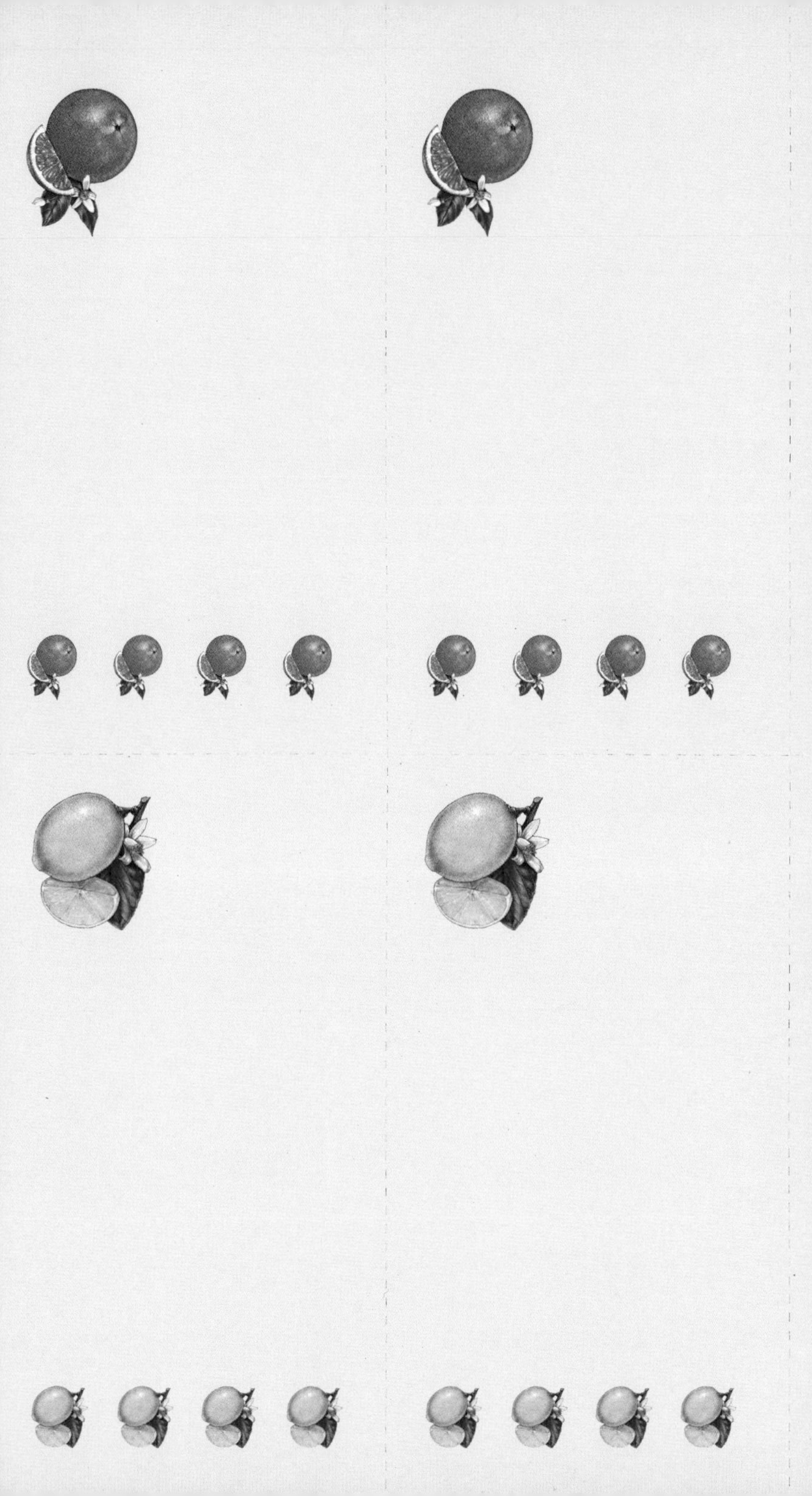

Applesauce-Spice Bread

- 1 jar Applesauce-Spice Bread Mix
- 1½ cups applesauce
- 6 tablespoons shortening
- 2 eggs
- 1½ teaspoons vanilla
- Powdered sugar (optional)

1. Preheat oven to 350°F. Spray 9-inch square baking pan with nonstick cooking spray.

2. Pour contents of jar into large bowl. Add applesauce, shortening, eggs and vanilla; beat with electric mixer at low speed 30 seconds. Increase speed to medium; beat 2 minutes until batter is well blended. Pour into prepared pan.

3. Bake 40 to 45 minutes or until toothpick inserted into center comes out clean. Cool in pan on wire rack 15 minutes. Sprinkle with powdered sugar, if desired.

Makes 9 servings

Applesauce-Spice Bread

- 1 jar Applesauce-Spice Bread Mix
- 1½ cups applesauce
- 6 tablespoons shortening
- 2 eggs
- 1½ teaspoons vanilla
- Powdered sugar (optional)

1. Preheat oven to 350°F. Spray 9-inch square baking pan with nonstick cooking spray.

2. Pour contents of jar into large bowl. Add applesauce, shortening, eggs and vanilla; beat with electric mixer at low speed 30 seconds. Increase speed to medium; beat 2 minutes until batter is well blended. Pour into prepared pan.

3. Bake 40 to 45 minutes or until toothpick inserted into center comes out clean. Cool in pan on wire rack 15 minutes. Sprinkle with powdered sugar, if desired.

Makes 9 servings

English-Style Scones

- 1 jar English-Style Scone Mix
- 6 tablespoons cold butter
- 4 eggs, divided
- ¾ cup heavy cream
- 2 teaspoons vanilla
- 1 teaspoon water

1. Preheat oven to 375°F. Grease two cookie sheets.

2. Pour contents of jar into large bowl. Add butter; blend with pastry blender or two knives until mixture resembles coarse crumbs. Beat 3 eggs, cream and vanilla in small bowl. Add to flour mixture; mix just until ingredients are moistened. Knead dough several times on lightly floured surface. Divide dough in half; place each half on prepared cookie sheet and pat into 6-inch circle (about 1 inch thick).

3. With sharp, wet knife, gently score each circle of dough into six wedges, cutting ¾ of the way into dough. Beat remaining egg with water; brush lightly over dough. Bake 18 to 20 minutes or until golden brown. Cool 5 minutes on wire rack. Cut into wedges. Serve warm with marmalade and whipped cream.

Makes 12 scones

English-Style Scones

- 1 jar English-Style Scone Mix
- 6 tablespoons cold butter
- 4 eggs, divided
- ¾ cup heavy cream
- 2 teaspoons vanilla
- 1 teaspoon water

1. Preheat oven to 375°F. Grease two cookie sheets.

2. Pour contents of jar into large bowl. Add butter; blend with pastry blender or two knives until mixture resembles coarse crumbs. Beat 3 eggs, cream and vanilla in small bowl. Add to flour mixture; mix just until ingredients are moistened. Knead dough several times on lightly floured surface. Divide dough in half; place each half on prepared cookie sheet and pat into 6-inch circle (about 1 inch thick).

3. With sharp, wet knife, gently score each circle of dough into six wedges, cutting ¾ of the way into dough. Beat remaining egg with water; brush lightly over dough. Bake 18 to 20 minutes or until golden brown. Cool 5 minutes on wire rack. Cut into wedges. Serve warm with marmalade and whipped cream.

Makes 12 scones

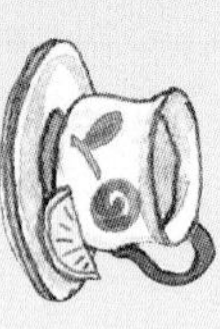

Currant Scones

1 jar Currant Scone Mix
¾ cup (1½ sticks) chilled butter, cut into small pieces
1 cup buttermilk
1 tablespoon grated fresh orange peel (optional)

1. Preheat oven to 425°F. Lightly grease two cookie sheets.

2. Pour contents of jar into large bowl. Cut in butter with pastry blender or two knives until mixture resembles coarse crumbs. Stir in buttermilk and orange peel, if desired. Stir until mixture forms soft dough that clings together. (Dough will be tacky.)

3. Lightly flour hands; divide dough in half and shape each half into a ball. Pat each ball into 8-inch circle on prepared cookie sheets. Score each circle into 8 wedges with floured knife, cutting about ¾ of the way into dough. Bake 16 to 18 minutes or until lightly browned. Cut into wedges; serve warm.

Makes 16 scones

Chocolate Macadamia Nut Muffins

1 jar Chocolate Macadamia Nut Muffin Mix
1 cup buttermilk
⅓ cup butter, melted
2 eggs
1½ teaspoons vanilla
Powdered sugar (optional)

1. Preheat oven to 400°F. Grease or paper-line 18 regular-size (2½-inch) muffin cups.

2. Pour contents of jar into large bowl. Combine buttermilk, butter, eggs and vanilla in small bowl until blended; stir into jar mixture just until moistened. Spoon evenly into prepared muffin cups.

3. Bake 13 to 17 minutes or until toothpick inserted into centers comes out clean. Cool in pans on wire racks 5 minutes; remove from pans and cool completely on wire racks. Sprinkle with powdered sugar, if desired.

Makes 18 muffins

Currant Scones

1 jar Currant Scone Mix
¾ cup (1½ sticks) chilled butter, cut into small pieces
1 cup buttermilk
1 tablespoon grated fresh orange peel (optional)

1. Preheat oven to 425°F. Lightly grease two cookie sheets.

2. Pour contents of jar into large bowl. Cut in butter with pastry blender or two knives until mixture resembles coarse crumbs. Stir in buttermilk and orange peel, if desired. Stir until mixture forms soft dough that clings together. (Dough will be tacky.)

3. Lightly flour hands; divide dough in half and shape each half into a ball. Pat each ball into 8-inch circle on prepared cookie sheets. Score each circle into 8 wedges with floured knife, cutting about ¾ of the way into dough. Bake 16 to 18 minutes or until lightly browned. Cut into wedges; serve warm.

Makes 16 scones

Chocolate Macadamia Nut Muffins

1 jar Chocolate Macadamia Nut Muffin Mix
1 cup buttermilk
⅓ cup butter, melted
2 eggs
1½ teaspoons vanilla
Powdered sugar (optional)

1. Preheat oven to 400°F. Grease or paper-line 18 regular-size (2½-inch) muffin cups.

2. Pour contents of jar into large bowl. Combine buttermilk, butter, eggs and vanilla in small bowl until blended; stir into jar mixture just until moistened. Spoon evenly into prepared muffin cups.

3. Bake 13 to 17 minutes or until toothpick inserted into centers comes out clean. Cool in pans on wire racks 5 minutes; remove from pans and cool completely on wire racks. Sprinkle with powdered sugar, if desired.

Makes 18 muffins

Recipes
Recipes

Apple Raisin Muffins

- **1 jar Apple Raisin Muffin Mix**
- **½ cup milk**
- **½ cup (1 stick) butter, melted**
- **2 eggs**

1. Preheat oven to 400°F. Grease or paper-line 12 regular-size (2½-inch) muffin cups.

2. Pour contents of jar into large bowl. Combine milk, butter and eggs in small bowl until blended; stir into jar mixture just until moistened. Spoon evenly into prepared muffin cups, filling about ⅔ full.

3. Bake 15 to 17 minutes or until toothpick inserted into centers comes out clean. Remove from pan and cool on wire rack.

Makes 12 muffins

Strawberry Muffins

- **1 jar Strawberry Muffin Mix**
- **1½ cups milk**
- **¾ cup (1½ sticks) butter, melted**
- **2 eggs, beaten**
- **1½ teaspoons vanilla**
- **2 cups chopped fresh or frozen strawberries (thaw and drain before using)**

1. Preheat oven to 400°F. Grease or paper-line 18 regular-size (2½-inch) muffin cups.

2. Pour contents of jar into large bowl. Combine milk, butter, eggs and vanilla in small bowl until blended; stir into jar mixture just until moistened. Gently fold in strawberries. Spoon batter evenly into prepared muffin cups, filling almost full.

3. Bake 15 to 17 minutes or until toothpick inserted into centers comes out clean. Remove from pans and cool 10 minutes on wire racks. Serve warm or cool completely.

Makes 18 muffins

Apple Raisin Muffins

- **1 jar Apple Raisin Muffin Mix**
- **½ cup milk**
- **½ cup (1 stick) butter, melted**
- **2 eggs**

1. Preheat oven to 400°F. Grease or paper-line 12 regular-size (2½-inch) muffin cups.

2. Pour contents of jar into large bowl. Combine milk, butter and eggs in small bowl until blended; stir into jar mixture just until moistened. Spoon evenly into prepared muffin cups, filling about ⅔ full.

3. Bake 15 to 17 minutes or until toothpick inserted into centers comes out clean. Remove from pan and cool on wire rack.

Makes 12 muffins

Strawberry Muffins

- **1 jar Strawberry Muffin Mix**
- **1½ cups milk**
- **¾ cup (1½ sticks) butter, melted**
- **2 eggs, beaten**
- **1½ teaspoons vanilla**
- **2 cups chopped fresh or frozen strawberries (thaw and drain before using)**

1. Preheat oven to 400°F. Grease or paper-line 18 regular-size (2½-inch) muffin cups.

2. Pour contents of jar into large bowl. Combine milk, butter, eggs and vanilla in small bowl until blended; stir into jar mixture just until moistened. Gently fold in strawberries. Spoon batter evenly into prepared muffin cups, filling almost full.

3. Bake 15 to 17 minutes or until toothpick inserted into centers comes out clean. Remove from pans and cool 10 minutes on wire racks. Serve warm or cool completely.

Makes 18 muffins

Pumpkin Chocolate Chip Muffins

1 jar Pumpkin Chocolate Chip Muffin Mix
1 cup canned pumpkin
3/4 cup milk
6 tablespoons butter, melted
2 eggs

1. Preheat oven to 400°F. Grease or paper-line 18 regular-size (2½-inch) muffin cups.

2. Pour contents of jar into large bowl. Combine pumpkin, milk, butter and eggs in small bowl until blended; stir into jar mixture just until moistened. Spoon evenly into prepared muffin cups, filling ⅔ full.

3. Bake 15 to 17 minutes or until toothpick inserted into centers comes out clean. Cool in pans on wire racks 10 minutes; remove from pan and cool completely on wire racks.

Makes 18 muffins

Apricot-Cranberry Bread

1 jar Apricot-Cranberry Bread Mix
1¼ cups buttermilk
¼ cup shortening
1 egg, beaten

1. Preheat oven to 350°F. Spray 9×5-inch loaf pan with nonstick cooking spray.

2. Pour contents of jar into large bowl. Combine buttermilk, shortening and egg in small bowl until blended; stir into jar mixture just until moistened. Pour evenly into prepared pan.

3. Bake 45 to 50 minutes or until toothpick inserted into center comes out clean. Cool in pan on wire rack 10 minutes; remove from pan and cool completely on wire rack.

Makes 1 loaf

Pumpkin Chocolate Chip Muffins

1 jar Pumpkin Chocolate Chip Muffin Mix
1 cup canned pumpkin
3/4 cup milk
6 tablespoons butter, melted
2 eggs

1. Preheat oven to 400°F. Grease or paper-line 18 regular-size (2½-inch) muffin cups.

2. Pour contents of jar into large bowl. Combine pumpkin, milk, butter and eggs in small bowl until blended; stir into jar mixture just until moistened. Spoon evenly into prepared muffin cups, filling ⅔ full.

3. Bake 15 to 17 minutes or until toothpick inserted into centers comes out clean. Cool in pans on wire racks 10 minutes; remove from pan and cool completely on wire racks.

Makes 18 muffins

Apricot-Cranberry Bread

1 jar Apricot-Cranberry Bread Mix
1¼ cups buttermilk
¼ cup shortening
1 egg, beaten

1. Preheat oven to 350°F. Spray 9×5-inch loaf pan with nonstick cooking spray.

2. Pour contents of jar into large bowl. Combine buttermilk, shortening and egg in small bowl until blended; stir into jar mixture just until moistened. Pour evenly into prepared pan.

3. Bake 45 to 50 minutes or until toothpick inserted into center comes out clean. Cool in pan on wire rack 10 minutes; remove from pan and cool completely on wire rack.

Makes 1 loaf

Peanut Butter Chocolate Chip Loaves

- **1 cup creamy peanut butter**
- **½ cup (1 stick) butter, softened**
- **2 eggs**
- **2 teaspoons vanilla**
- **1 jar Peanut Butter Chocolate Chip Loaves Mix**
- **1½ cups buttermilk**

1. Preheat oven to 350°F. Spray two 8½×4½-inch loaf pans with nonstick cooking spray.

2. Beat peanut butter and butter in large bowl with electric mixer at medium speed until light and fluffy. Beat in eggs, one at a time, beating well after each addition. Beat in vanilla. Add contents of jar alternately with buttermilk, beating at low speed after each addition until blended. Divide batter evenly between prepared pans.

3. Bake about 45 minutes or until toothpick inserted into centers comes out clean. Cool in pans on wire racks 10 minutes. Remove from pans and cool completely on wire racks.

Makes 2 loaves

Peanut Butter Chocolate Chip Loaves

- **1 cup creamy peanut butter**
- **½ cup (1 stick) butter, softened**
- **2 eggs**
- **2 teaspoons vanilla**
- **1 jar Peanut Butter Chocolate Chip Loaves Mix**
- **1½ cups buttermilk**

1. Preheat oven to 350°F. Spray two 8½×4½-inch loaf pans with nonstick cooking spray.

2. Beat peanut butter and butter in large bowl with electric mixer at medium speed until light and fluffy. Beat in eggs, one at a time, beating well after each addition. Beat in vanilla. Add contents of jar alternately with buttermilk, beating at low speed after each addition until blended. Divide batter evenly between prepared pans.

3. Bake about 45 minutes or until toothpick inserted into centers comes out clean. Cool in pans on wire racks 10 minutes. Remove from pans and cool completely on wire racks.

Makes 2 loaves

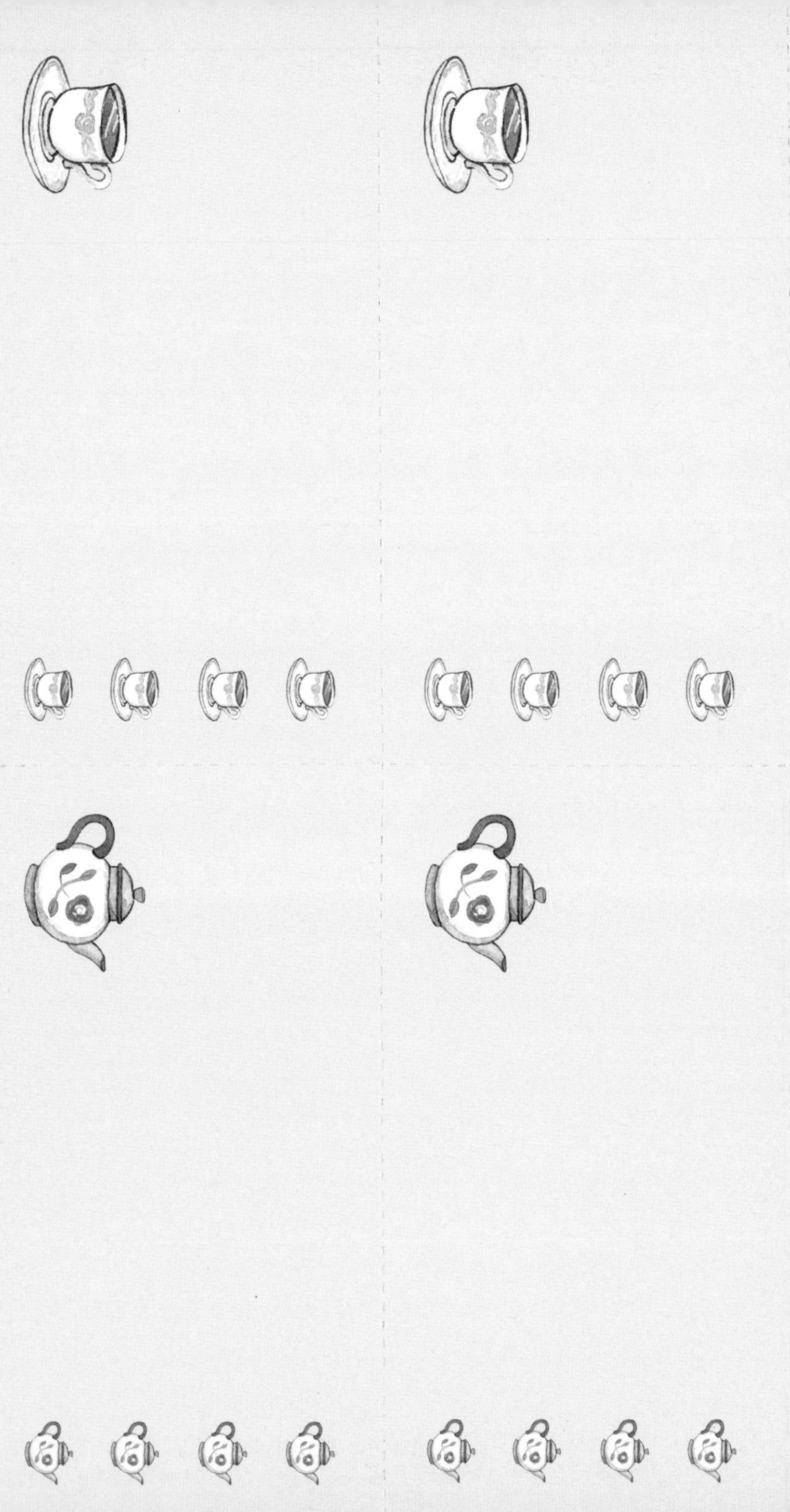

Applesauce-Spice Bread Mix

- 2¼ cups all-purpose flour
- 1 cup plus 2 tablespoons packed light brown sugar
- ¾ cup raisins
- ½ cup toasted chopped walnuts
- 1¼ teaspoons baking soda
- 1 teaspoon ground cinnamon
- ½ teaspoon salt
- ½ teaspoon baking powder
- ¼ teaspoon ground nutmeg

1. Layer ingredients attractively in any order in 1-quart food storage jar with tight-fitting lid. Pack ingredients down slightly before adding another layer.

2. Cover top of jar with fabric; attach gift tag with raffia or ribbon.

Makes one (1-quart) jar

Applesauce-Spice Bread

- 1 jar Applesauce-Spice Bread Mix
- 1½ cups applesauce
- 6 tablespoons shortening
- 2 eggs
- 1½ teaspoons vanilla
- Powdered sugar (optional)

1. Preheat oven to 350°F. Spray 9-inch square baking pan with nonstick cooking spray.

2. Pour contents of jar into large bowl. Add applesauce, shortening, eggs and vanilla; beat with electric mixer at low speed 30 seconds. Increase speed to medium; beat 2 minutes until batter is well blended. Pour into prepared pan.

3. Bake 40 to 45 minutes or until toothpick inserted into center comes out clean. Cool in pan on wire rack. Sprinkle with powdered sugar, if desired.

Makes 9 servings

Chocolate Macadamia Nut Muffin Mix

- 2 cups all-purpose flour
- 1 cup sugar
- 1 cup chocolate chips
- ½ cup coarsely chopped macadamia nuts
- ¼ cup unsweetened cocoa powder
- 1½ teaspoons baking soda
- ½ teaspoon salt

1. Layer ingredients attractively in any order in 1-quart food storage jar with tight-fitting lid. Pack ingredients down slightly before adding another layer.

2. Cover top of jar with fabric; attach gift tag with raffia or ribbon.

Makes one (1-quart) jar

Chocolate Macadamia Nut Muffins

1 jar Chocolate Macadamia Nut Muffin Mix
1 cup buttermilk
⅓ cup butter, melted
2 eggs
1½ teaspoons vanilla
Powdered sugar (optional)

1. Preheat oven to 400°F. Grease or paper-line 18 regular-size (2½-inch) muffin cups.

2. Pour contents of jar into large bowl. Combine buttermilk, butter, eggs and vanilla in small bowl until blended; stir into jar mixture just until moistened. Spoon evenly into prepared muffin cups.

3. Bake 13 to 17 minutes or until toothpick inserted into centers comes out clean. Cool in pans on wire racks 5 minutes; remove from pans and cool completely on wire racks. Sprinkle with powdered sugar, if desired. *Makes 18 muffins*

Currant Scone Mix

3 cups all-purpose flour
½ cup sugar
2 teaspoons baking powder
½ teaspoon salt
½ teaspoon baking soda
1 cup currants

1. Layer ingredients attractively in any order in 1-quart food storage jar with tight-fitting lid.

2. Cover top of jar with fabric; attach gift tag with raffia or ribbon.

Makes one (1-quart) jar

Currant Scones

1 jar Currant Scone Mix
¾ cup (1½ sticks) chilled butter, cut into small pieces
1 cup buttermilk
1 tablespoon grated fresh orange peel (optional)

1. Preheat oven to 425°F. Lightly grease two cookie sheets.

2. Pour contents of jar into large bowl. Cut in butter with pastry blender or two knives until mixture resembles coarse crumbs. Stir in buttermilk and orange peel, if desired. Stir until mixture forms soft dough that clings together. (Dough will be tacky.)

3. Lightly flour hands; divide dough in half and shape each half into a ball. Pat each ball into 8-inch circle on prepared cookie sheets. Score each circle into 8 wedges with floured knife, cutting about ¾ of the way into dough. Bake 16 to 18 minutes or until lightly browned. Cut into wedges; serve warm. *Makes 16 scones*

Strawberry Muffin Mix

- 2 cups all-purpose flour
- 1½ cups uncooked old-fashioned oats
- ¾ cup sugar
- 3½ teaspoons baking powder
- ½ teaspoon salt
- ½ teaspoon ground cinnamon

1. Layer ingredients attractively in any order in 1-quart food storage jar with tight-fitting lid. Pack ingredients down slightly before adding another layer.

2. Cover top of jar with fabric; attach gift tag with raffia or ribbon.

Makes one (1-quart) jar

Strawberry Muffins

- 1 jar Strawberry Muffin Mix
- 1½ cups milk
- ¾ cup (1½ sticks) butter, melted
- 2 eggs, beaten
- 1½ teaspoons vanilla
- 2 cups chopped fresh or frozen strawberries (thaw and drain before using)

1. Preheat oven to 400°F. Grease or paper-line 18 regular-size (2½-inch) muffin cups.

2. Pour contents of jar into large bowl. Combine milk, butter, eggs and vanilla in small bowl until blended; stir into jar mixture just until moistened. Gently fold in strawberries. Spoon batter evenly into prepared muffin cups, filling almost full.

3. Bake 15 to 17 minutes or until toothpick inserted into centers comes out clean. Remove from pans and cool 10 minutes on wire racks. Serve warm or cool completely. *Makes 18 muffins*

Apple Raisin Muffin Mix

1½ cups all-purpose flour
1 cup chopped dried apples
⅔ cup packed brown sugar
½ cup uncooked old-fashioned oats
½ cup chopped walnuts
½ cup raisins
1 tablespoon baking powder
1 teaspoon ground cinnamon
½ teaspoon salt
⅛ teaspoon ground nutmeg
⅛ teaspoon ground ginger

1. Layer ingredients attractively in any order in 1-quart food storage jar with tight-fitting lid. Pack ingredients down slightly before adding another layer.

2. Cover top of jar with fabric; attach gift tag with raffia or ribbon.

Makes one (1-quart) jar

Apple Raisin Muffins

1 jar Apple Raisin Muffin Mix
½ cup milk
½ cup (1 stick) butter, melted
2 eggs

1. Preheat oven to 400°F. Grease or paper-line 12 regular-size (2½-inch) muffin cups.

2. Pour contents of jar into large bowl. Combine milk, butter and eggs in small bowl until blended; stir into jar mixture just until moistened. Spoon evenly into prepared muffin cups, filling about ⅔ full.

3. Bake 15 to 17 minutes or until toothpick inserted into centers comes out clean. Remove from pan and cool on wire rack.

Makes 12 muffins

Apricot-Cranberry Bread Mix

- 2½ cups all-purpose flour
- 1 cup chopped dried apricots
- ¾ cup sugar
- ½ cup dried cranberries
- 4 teaspoons baking powder
- ½ teaspoon baking soda
- ½ teaspoon salt

1. Layer ingredients attractively in any order in 1-quart food storage jar with tight-fitting lid. Pack ingredients down slightly before adding another layer.

2. Cover top of jar with fabric; attach gift tag with raffia or ribbon.

Makes one (1-quart) jar

Apricot-Cranberry Bread

1 jar Apricot-Cranberry Bread Mix
1¼ cups buttermilk
¼ cup shortening
1 egg, beaten

1. Preheat oven to 350°F. Spray 9×5-inch loaf pan with nonstick cooking spray.

2. Pour contents of jar into large bowl. Combine buttermilk, shortening and egg in small bowl until blended; stir into jar mixture just until moistened. Pour evenly into prepared pan.

3. Bake 45 to 50 minutes or until toothpick inserted into center comes out clean. Cool in pan on wire rack 10 minutes; remove from pan and cool completely on wire rack. *Makes 1 loaf*

Pumpkin Chocolate Chip Muffin Mix

- 2½ cups all-purpose flour
- 1 cup packed light brown sugar
- 1 cup chocolate chips
- ½ cup chopped walnuts
- 1 tablespoon baking powder
- 1½ teaspoons pumpkin pie spice
- ¼ teaspoon salt

1. Layer ingredients attractively in any order in 1-quart food storage jar with tight-fitting lid. Pack ingredients down slightly before adding another layer.

2. Cover top of jar with fabric; attach gift tag with raffia or ribbon.

Makes one (1-quart) jar

Pumpkin Chocolate Chip Muffins

1 jar Pumpkin Chocolate Chip Muffin Mix
1 cup canned pumpkin
¾ cup milk
6 tablespoons butter, melted
2 eggs

1. Preheat oven to 400°F. Grease or paper-line 18 regular-size (2½-inch) muffin cups.

2. Pour contents of jar into large bowl. Combine pumpkin, milk, butter and eggs in small bowl until blended; stir into jar mixture just until moistened. Spoon evenly into prepared muffin cups, filling ⅔ full.

3. Bake 15 to 17 minutes or until toothpick inserted into centers comes out clean. Cool in pans on wire racks 10 minutes; remove from pan and cool completely on wire racks. *Makes 18 muffins*

Peanut Butter Chocolate Chip Loaves Mix

- 3 cups all-purpose flour
- 1 cup semisweet mini chocolate chips
- ½ cup granulated sugar
- ½ cup packed light brown sugar
- 1½ teaspoons baking powder
- 1 teaspoon baking soda
- ½ teaspoon salt

1. Layer ingredients attractively in any order in 1-quart food storage jar with tight-fitting lid. Pack ingredients down slightly before adding another layer.

2. Cover top of jar with fabric; attach gift tag with raffia or ribbon.

Makes one (1-quart) jar

Peanut Butter Chocolate Chip Loaves

1 cup creamy peanut butter
½ cup (1 stick) butter, softened
2 eggs
2 teaspoons vanilla
1 jar Peanut Butter Chocolate Chip Loaves Mix
1½ cups buttermilk

1. Preheat oven to 350°F. Spray two 8½×4½-inch loaf pans with nonstick cooking spray.

2. Beat peanut butter and butter in large bowl with electric mixer at medium speed until light and fluffy. Beat in eggs, one at a time, beating well after each addition. Beat in vanilla. Add contents of jar alternately with buttermilk, beating at low speed after each addition until blended. Divide batter evenly between prepared pans.

3. Bake about 45 minutes or until toothpick inserted into centers comes out clean. Cool in pans on wire racks 10 minutes. Remove from pans and cool completely on wire racks. *Makes 2 loaves*